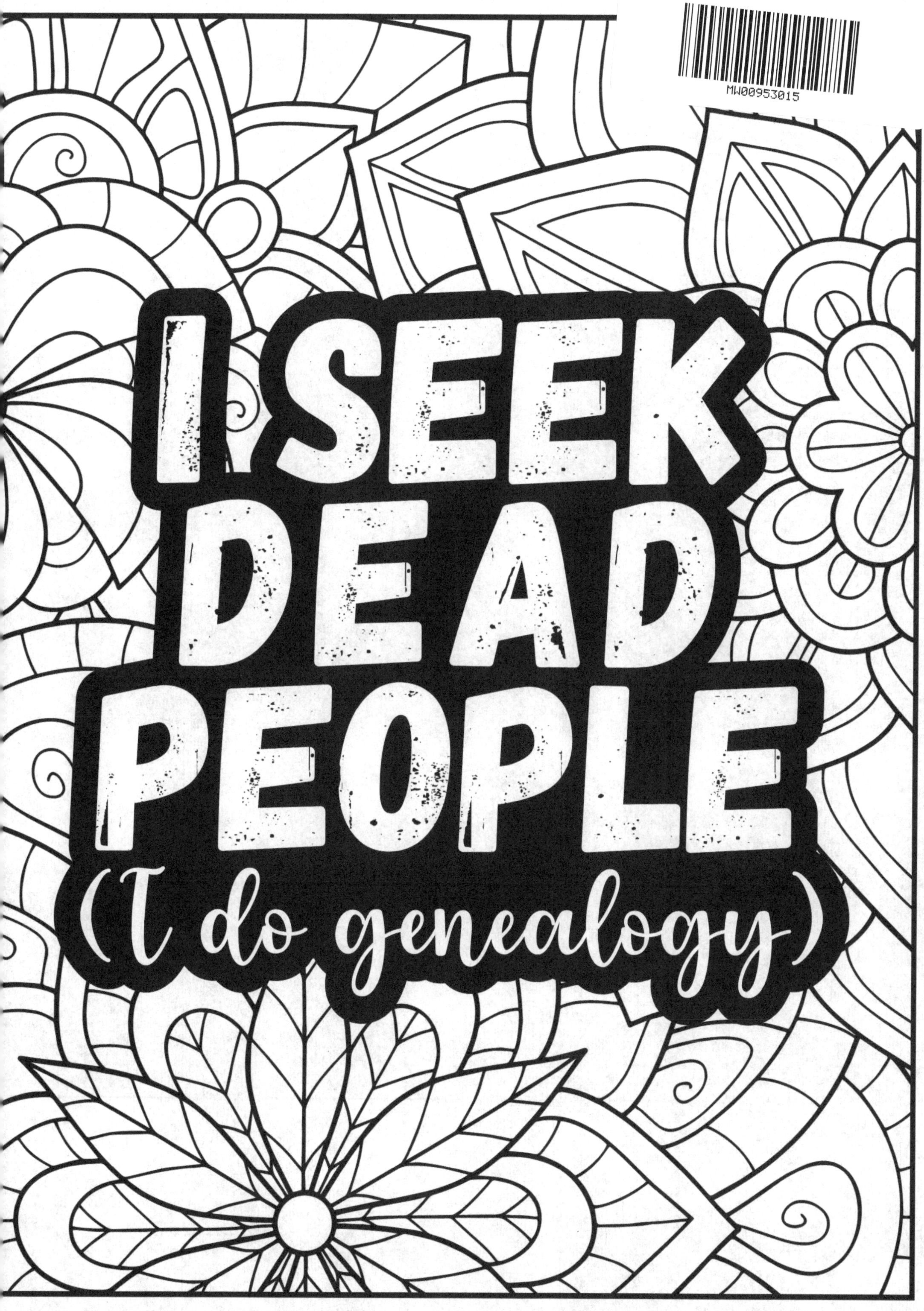
I SEEK
DEAD
PEOPLE
(I do genealogy)

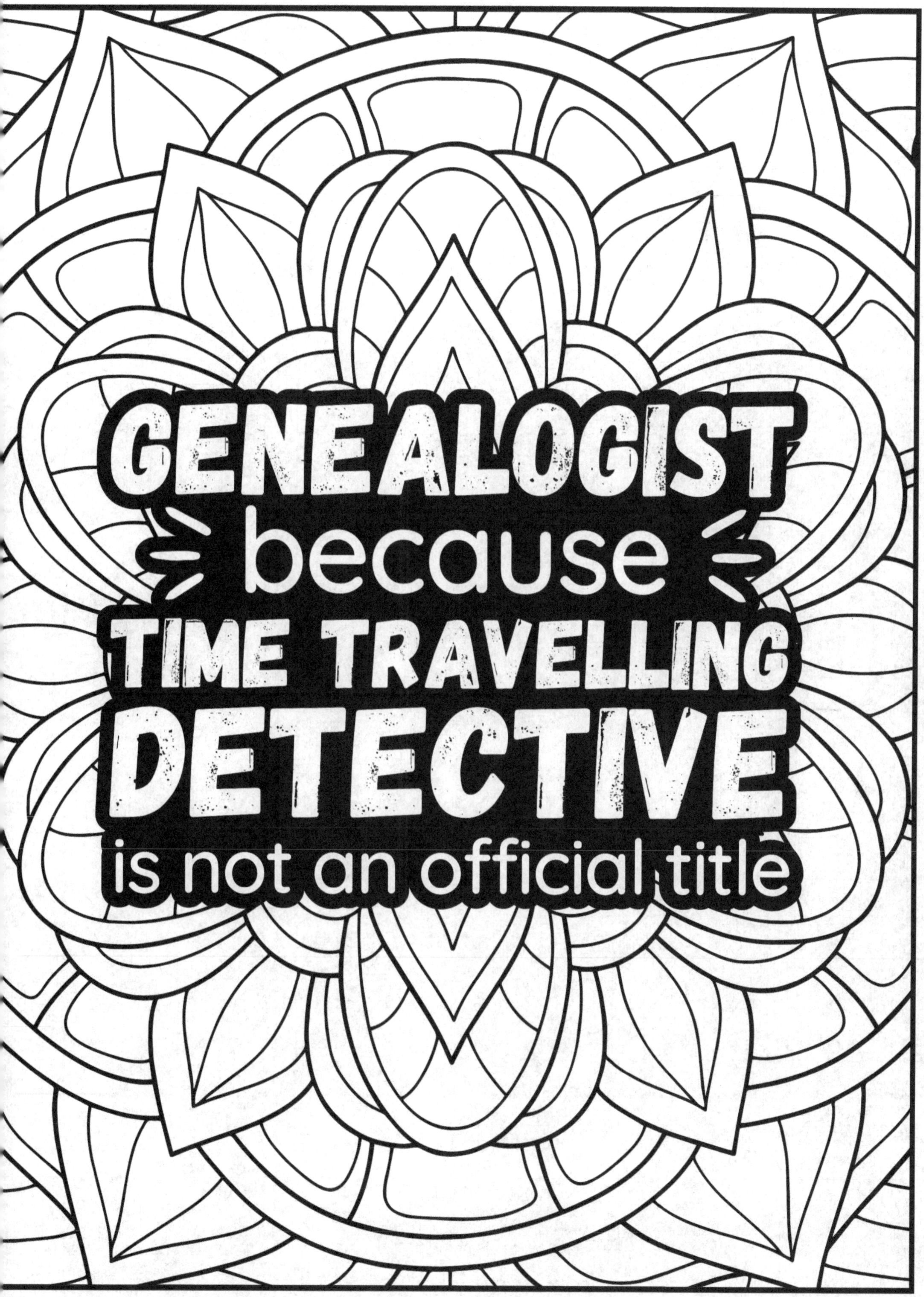
GENEALOGIST
because
TIME TRAVELLING
DETECTIVE
is not an official title

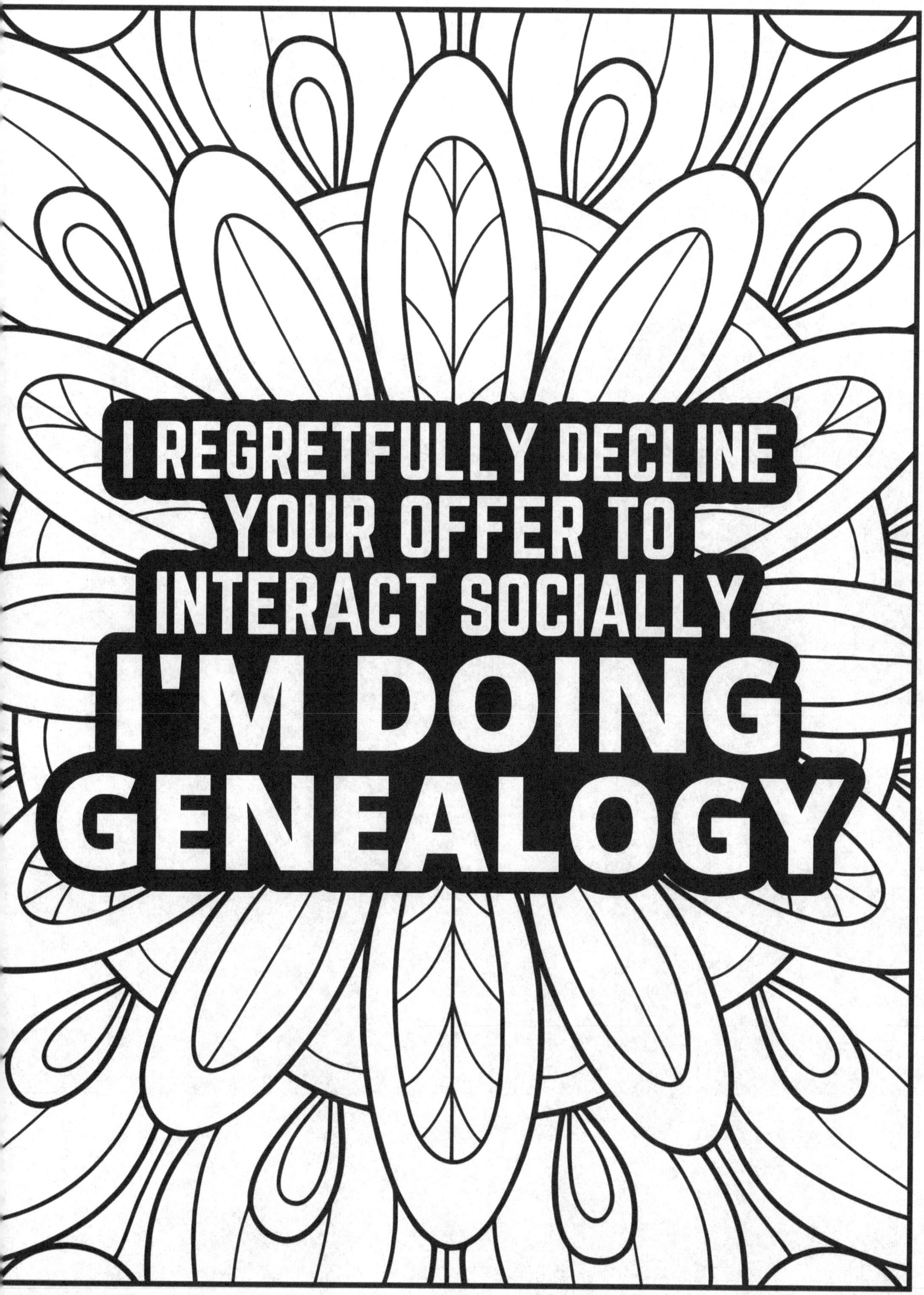
I REGRETFULLY DECLINE
YOUR OFFER TO
INTERACT SOCIALLY
I'M DOING
GENEALOGY

family
TREE
hugger

coffee
computer
genealogy
happy

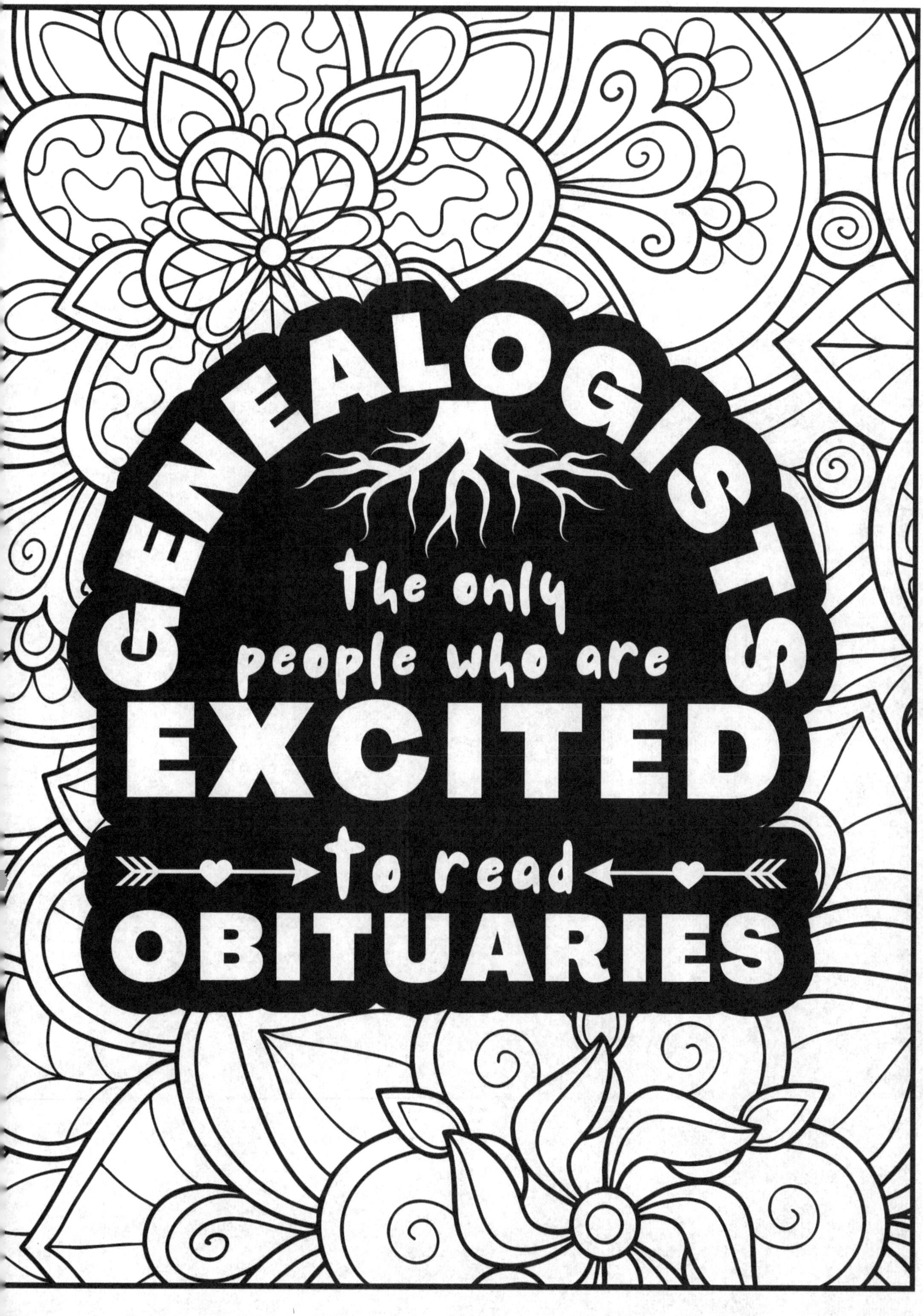
GENEALOGISTS
the only
people who are
EXCITED
to read
OBITUARIES

I'm tracing my
ANCESTORS
so I'll know
WHO TO BLAME

A DAY WITHOUT
genealogy
PROBABLY
WOULDN'T KILL ME
but why risk it?

I'M NOT STUCK
I'M
ANCESTRALLY
CHALLENGED

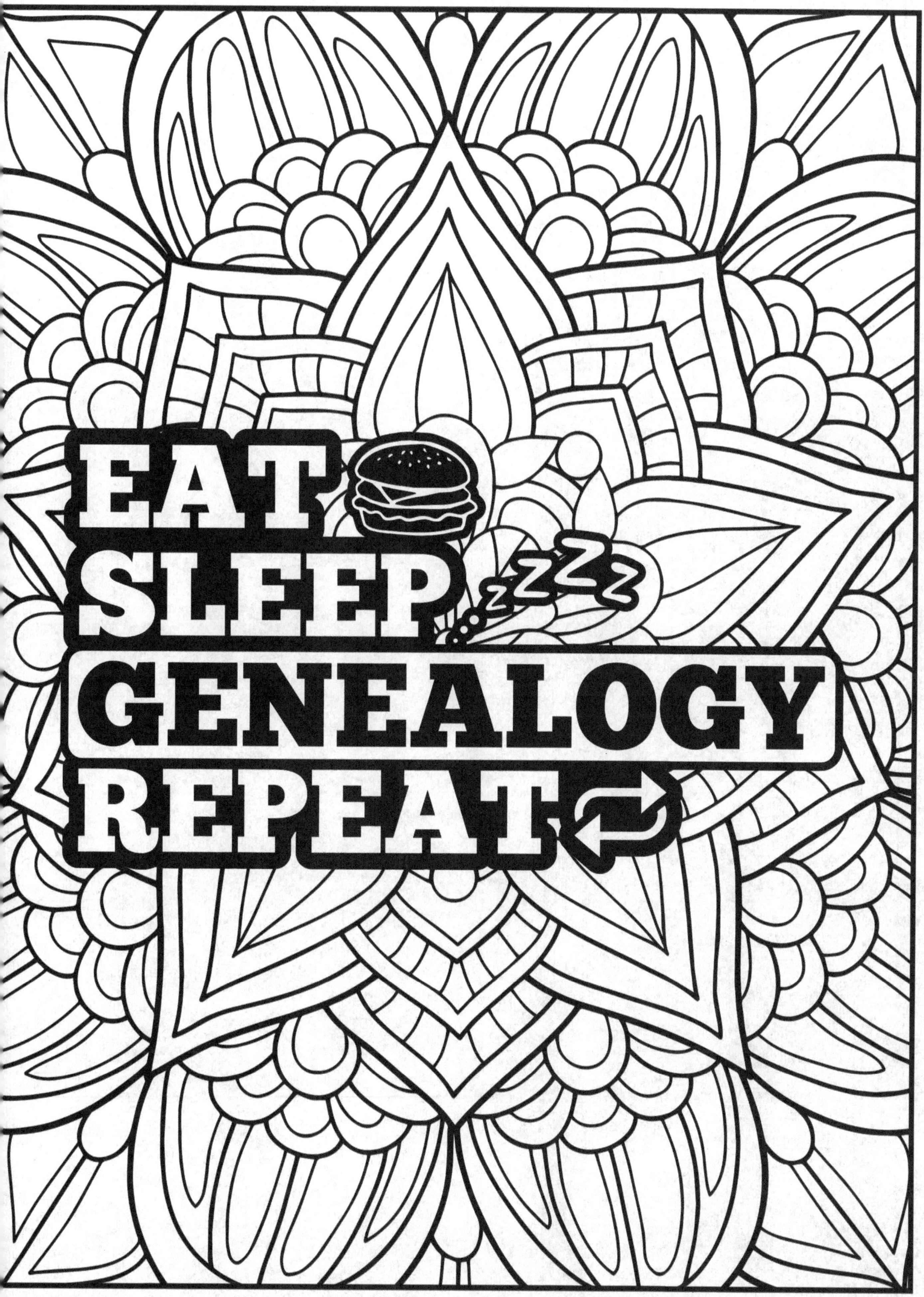
EAT
SLEEP
GENEALOGY
REPEAT

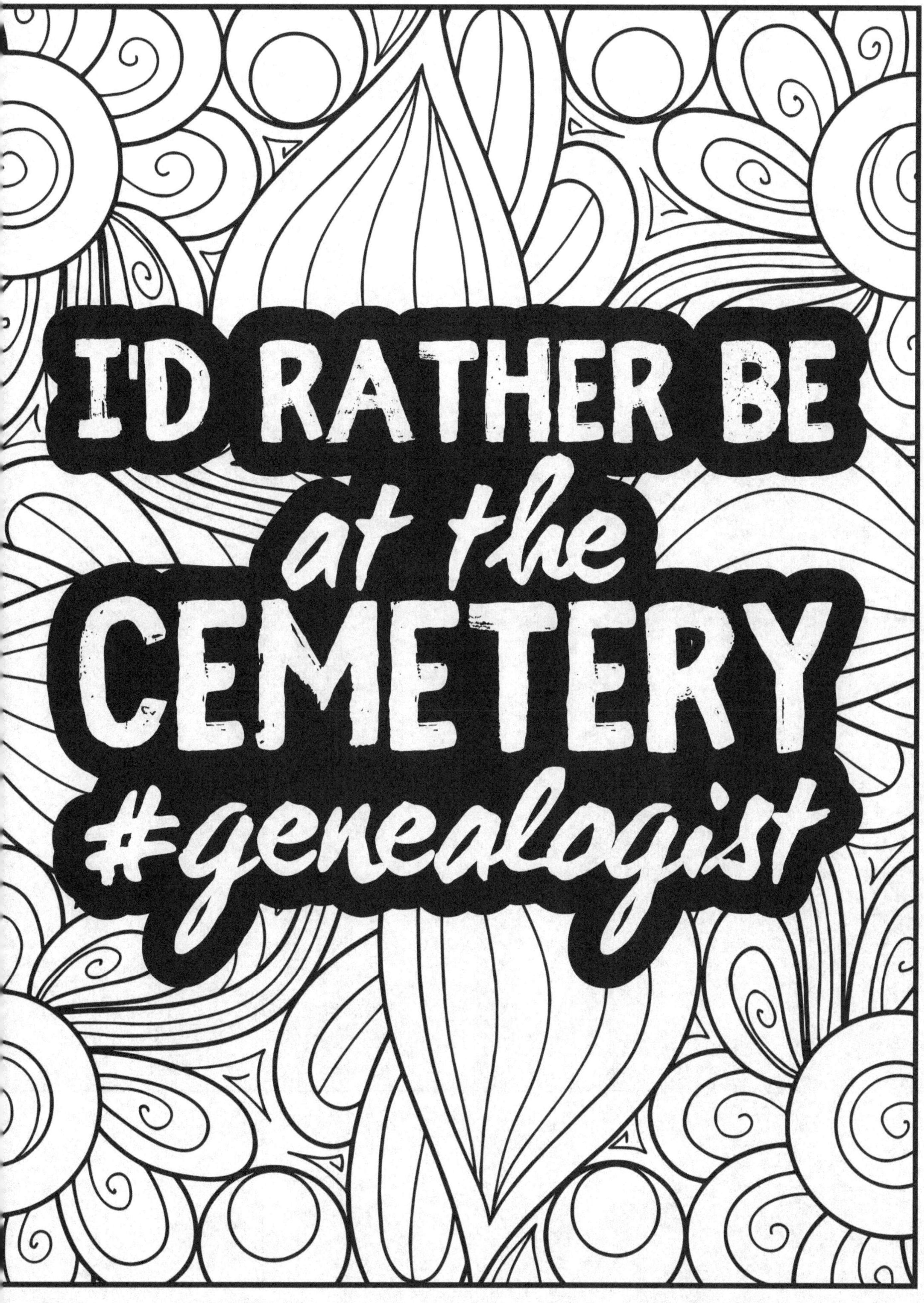
I'D RATHER BE
at the
CEMETERY
#genealogist

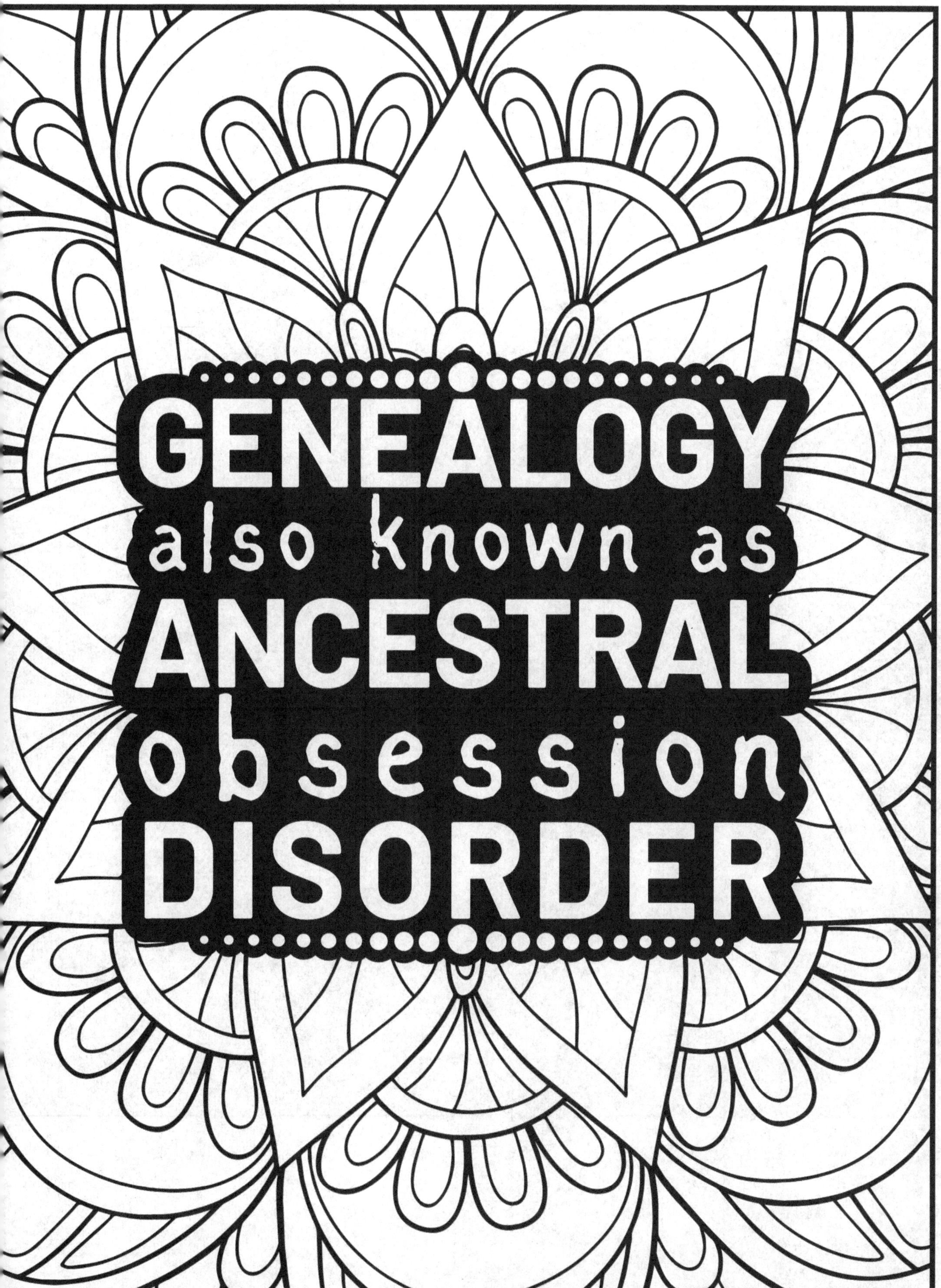
GENEALOGY
also known as
ANCESTRAL
obsession
DISORDER

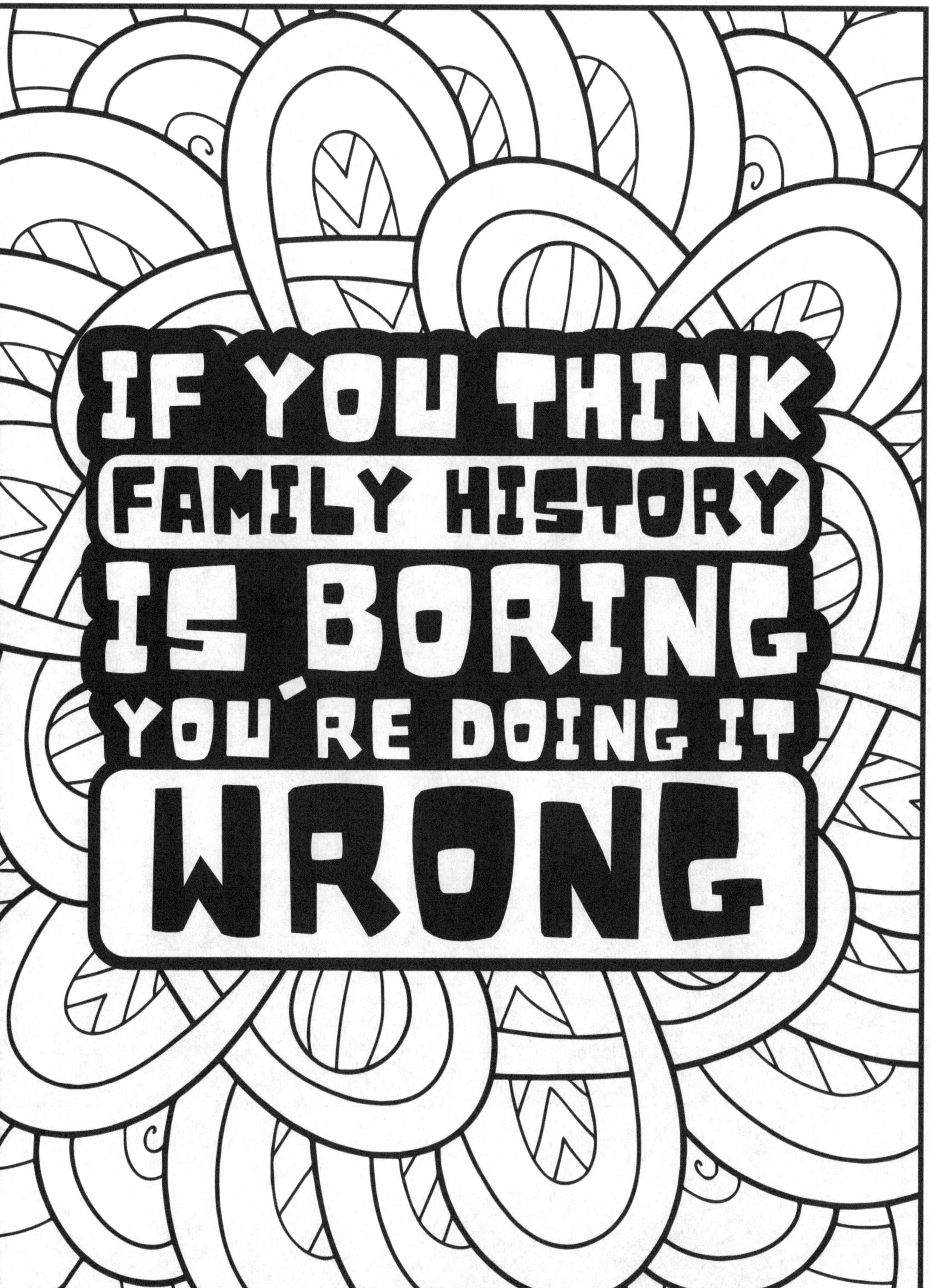
IF YOU THINK
FAMILY HISTORY
IS BORING
YOU'RE DOING IT
WRONG

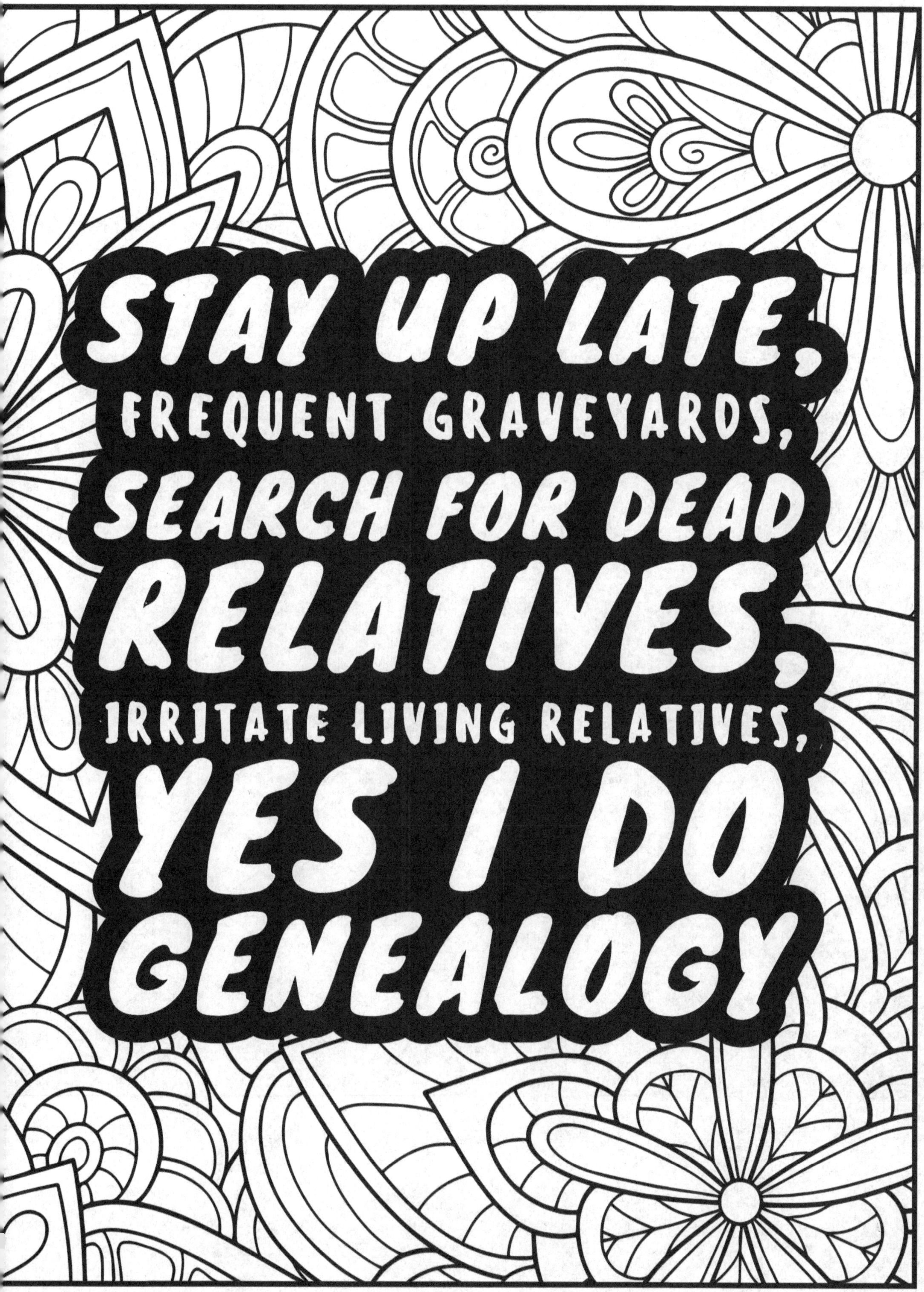
STAY UP LATE,
FREQUENT GRAVEYARDS,
SEARCH FOR DEAD
RELATIVES,
IRRITATE LIVING RELATIVES,
YES I DO
GENEALOGY

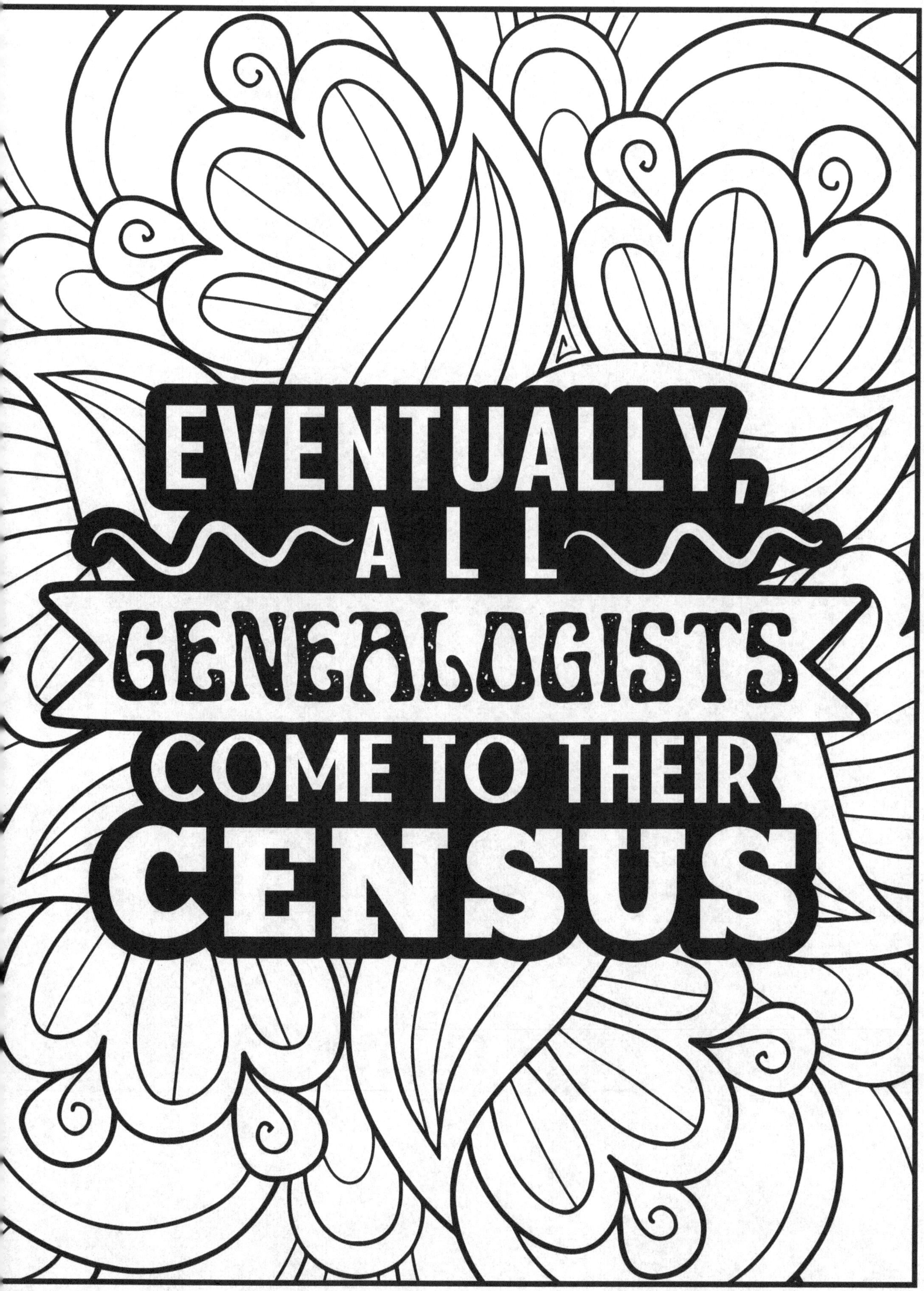
EVENTUALLY,
ALL
GENEALOGISTS
COME TO THEIR
CENSUS

Weekend
FORECAST
100% chance of
GENEALOGY

"MY WORK IS DONE.
I FOUND EVERYONE
IN MY FAMILY TREE
AND ALL MY DOCUMENTS
ARE ORGANIZED."
...SAID NO GENEALOGIST, EVER.

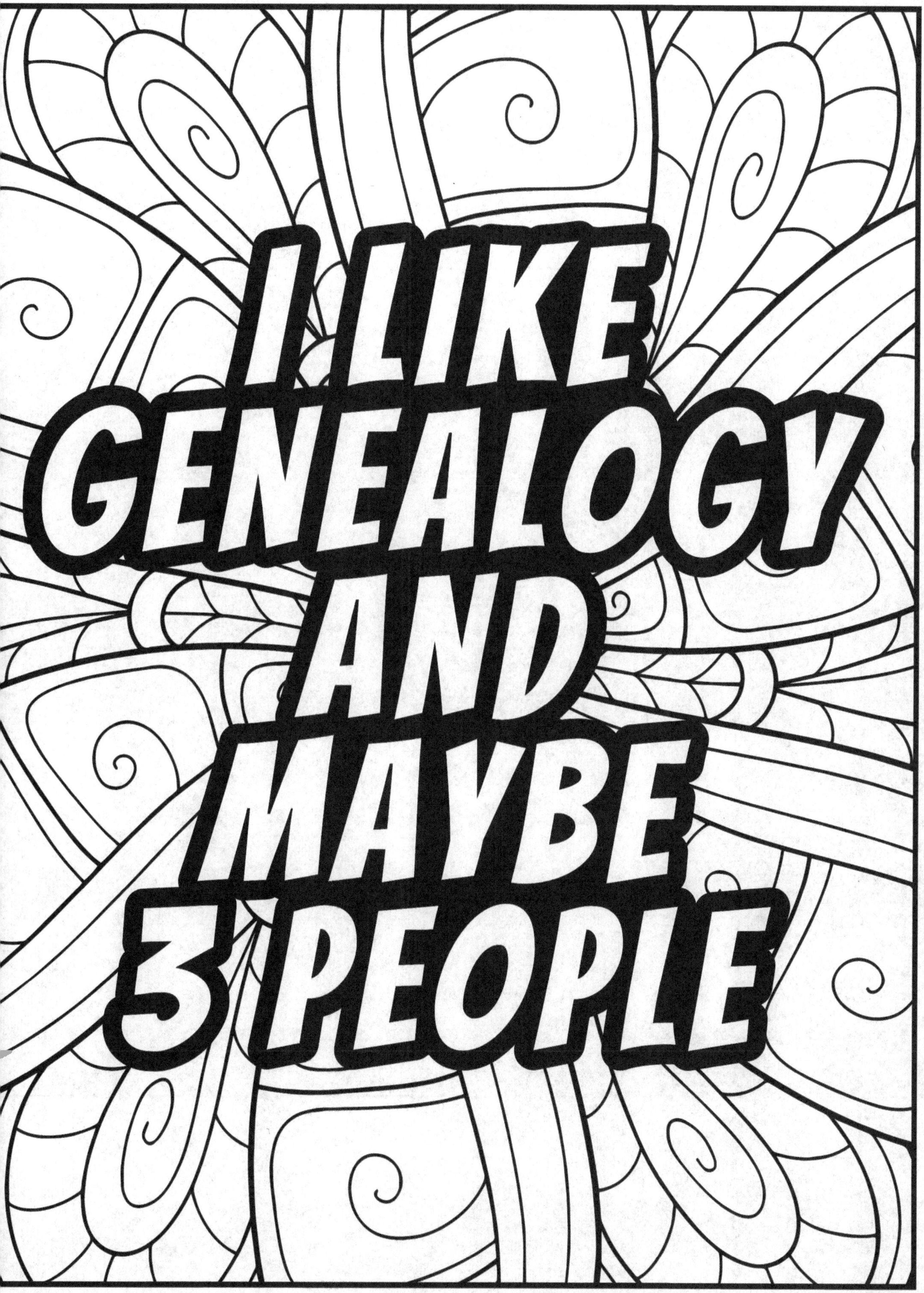
I LIKE
GENEALOGY
AND
MAYBE
3 PEOPLE

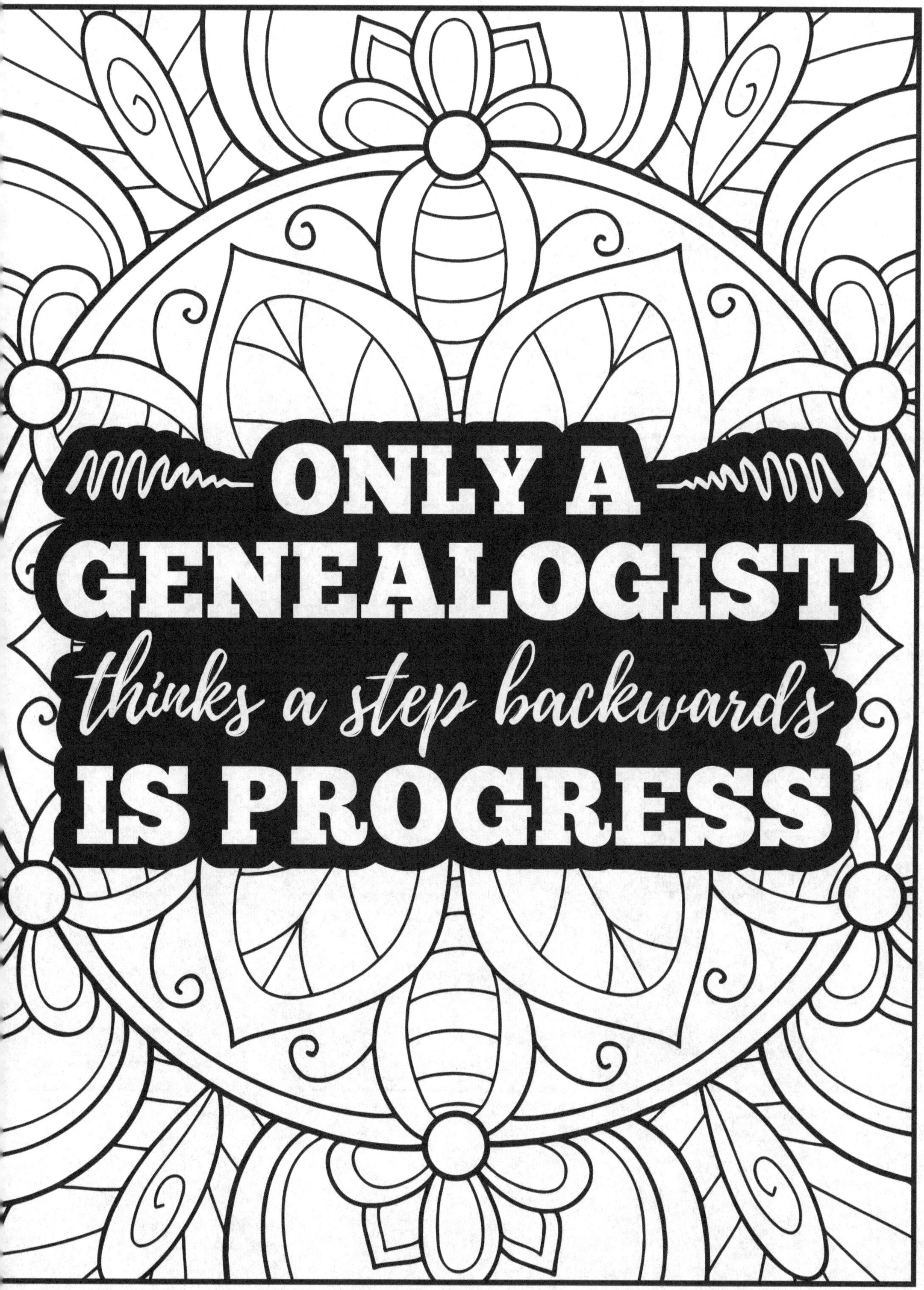
ONLY A
GENEALOGIST
thinks a step backwards
IS PROGRESS

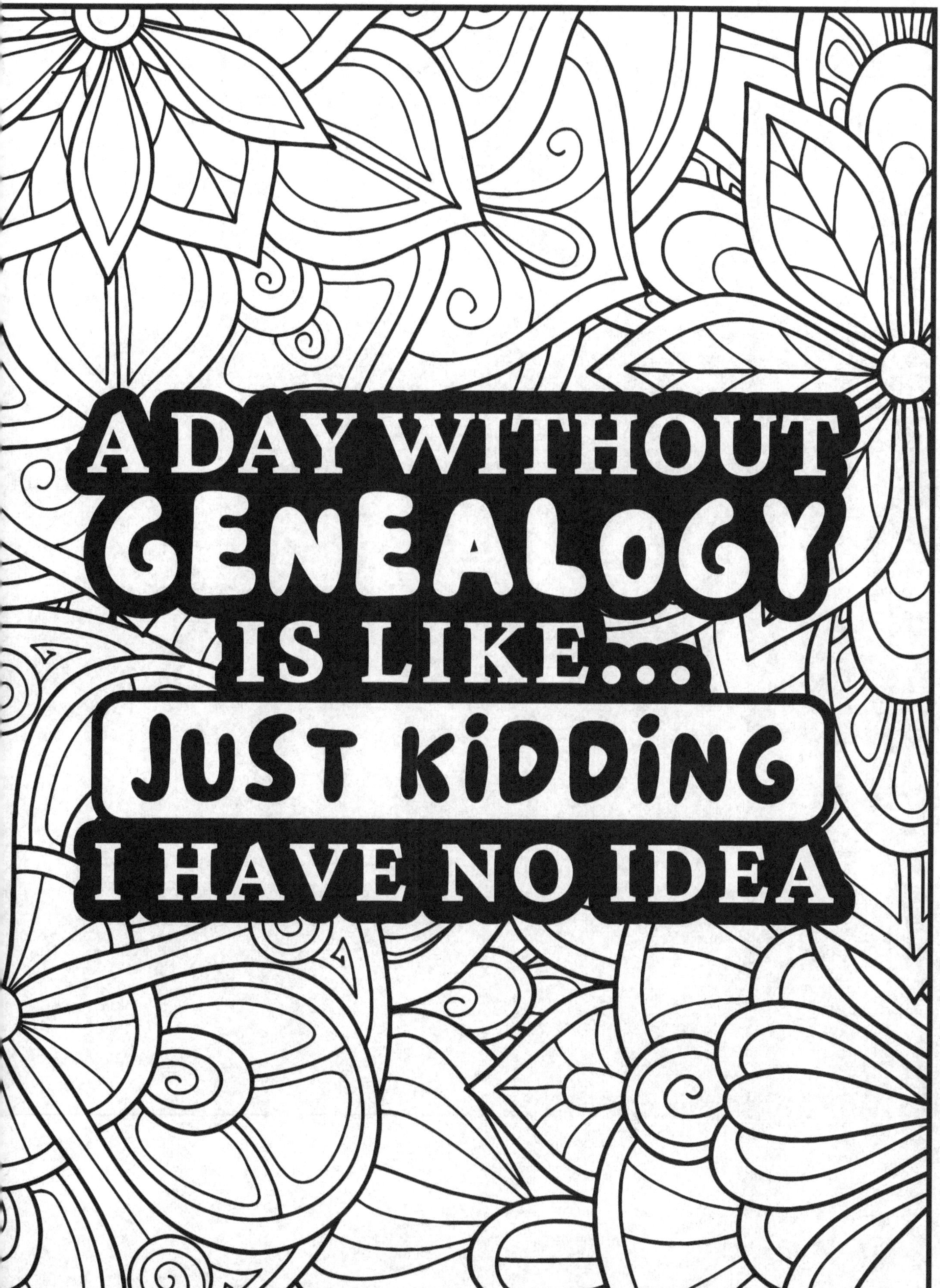
A DAY WITHOUT
GENEALOGY
IS LIKE...
JUST KIDDING
I HAVE NO IDEA

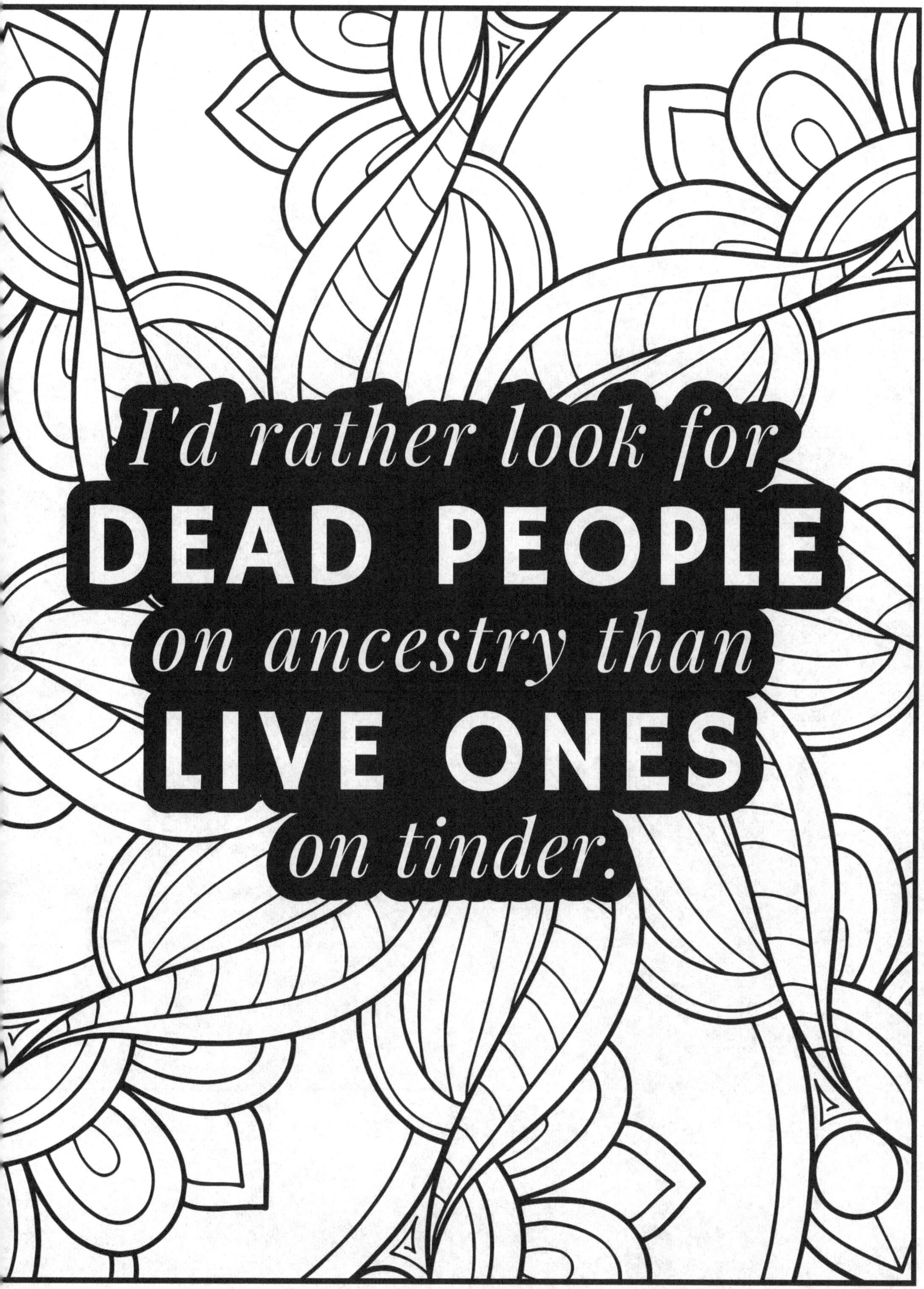
I'd rather look for
DEAD PEOPLE
on ancestry than
LIVE ONES
on tinder.

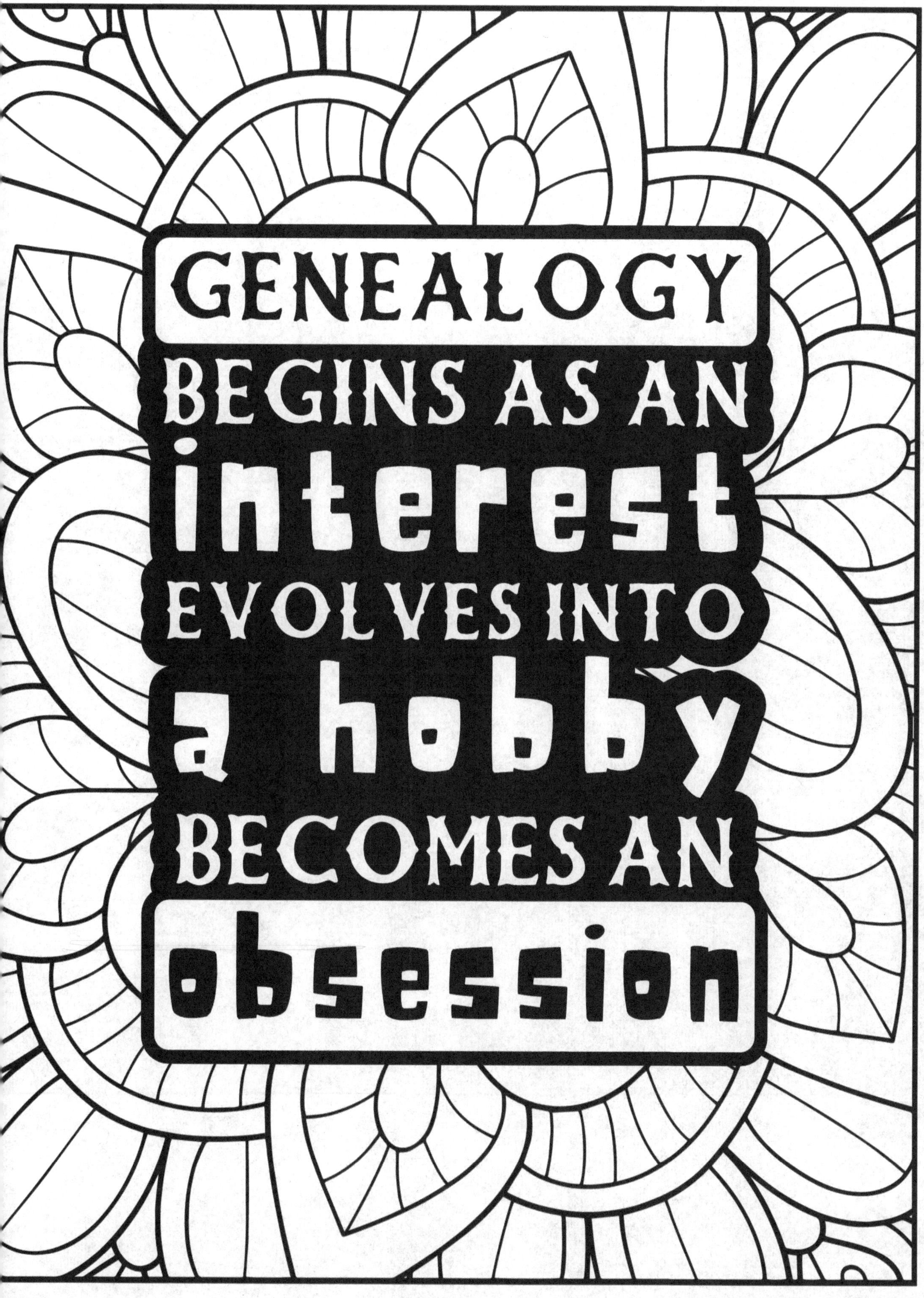
GENEALOGY
BEGINS AS AN
interest
EVOLVES INTO
a hobby
BECOMES AN
obsession

I collect DEAD relatives

GENEALOGY
REBEL
I RESEARCH
PAST MY BEDTIME

SO MANY
ancestors
SO LITTLE
time

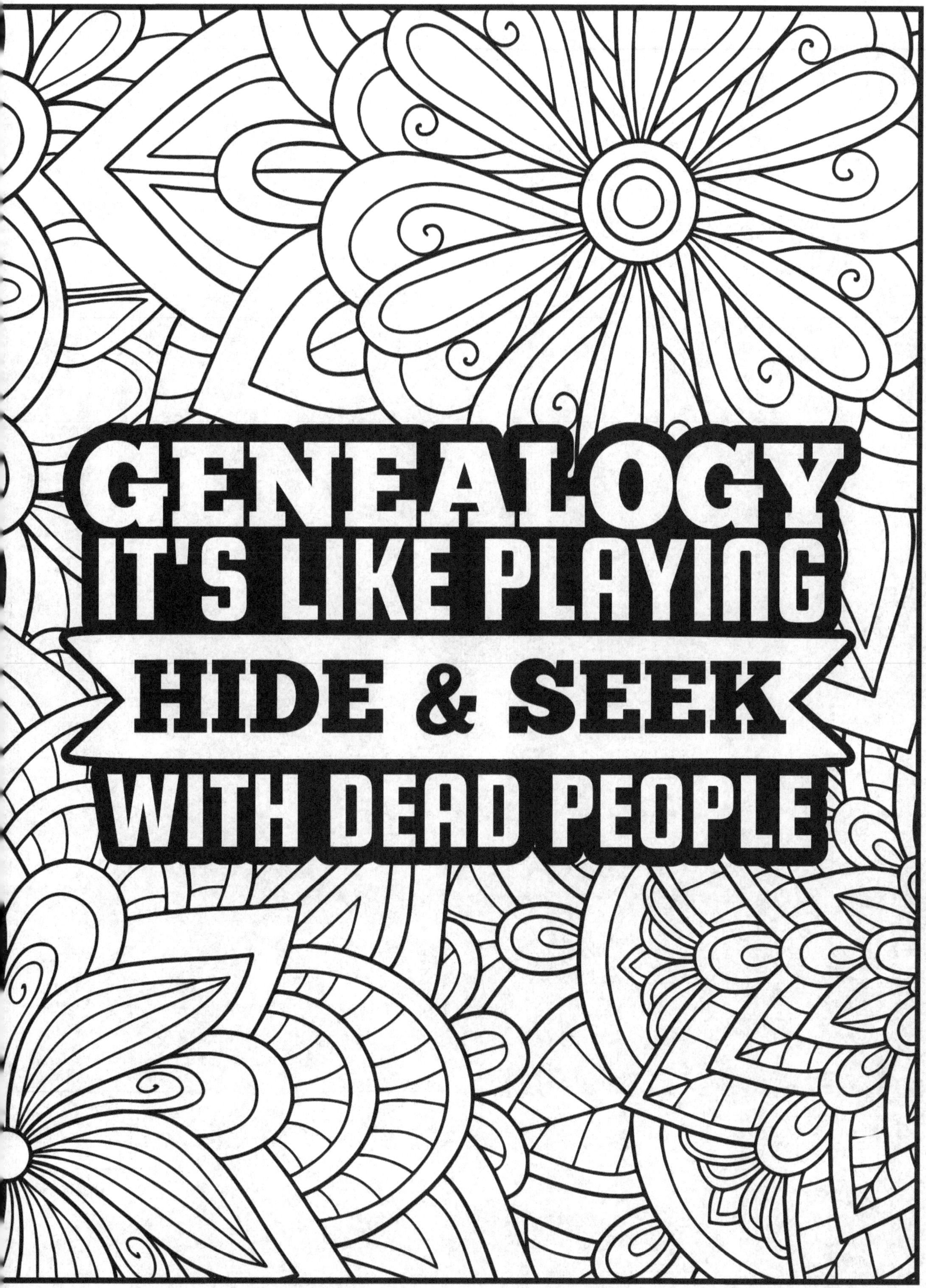
GENEALOGY
IT'S LIKE PLAYING
HIDE & SEEK
WITH DEAD PEOPLE

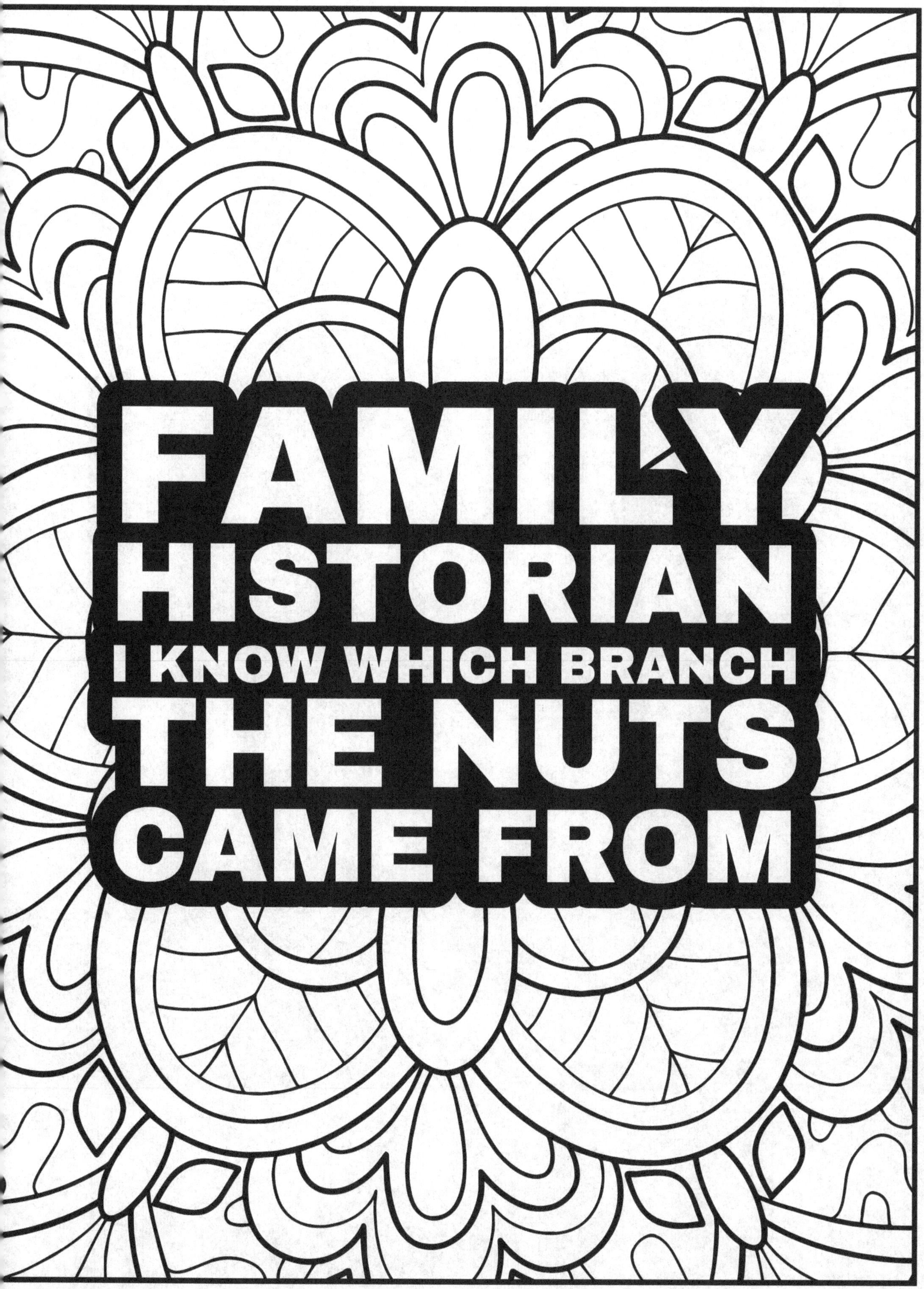
FAMILY
HISTORIAN
I KNOW WHICH BRANCH
THE NUTS
CAME FROM

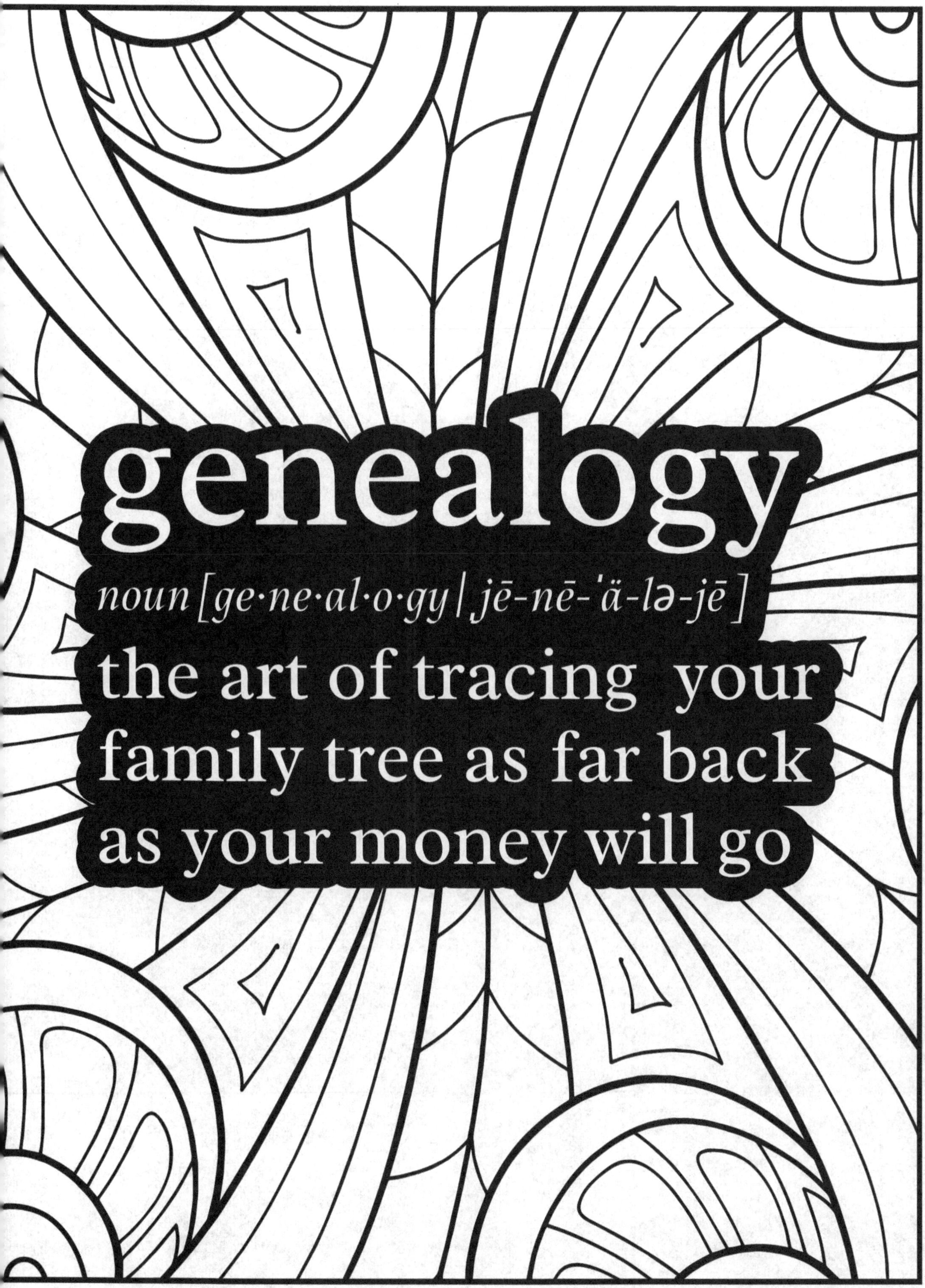
genealogy
noun [ge·ne·al·o·gy | jē-nē-ˈä-lə-jē]
the art of tracing your family tree as far back as your money will go

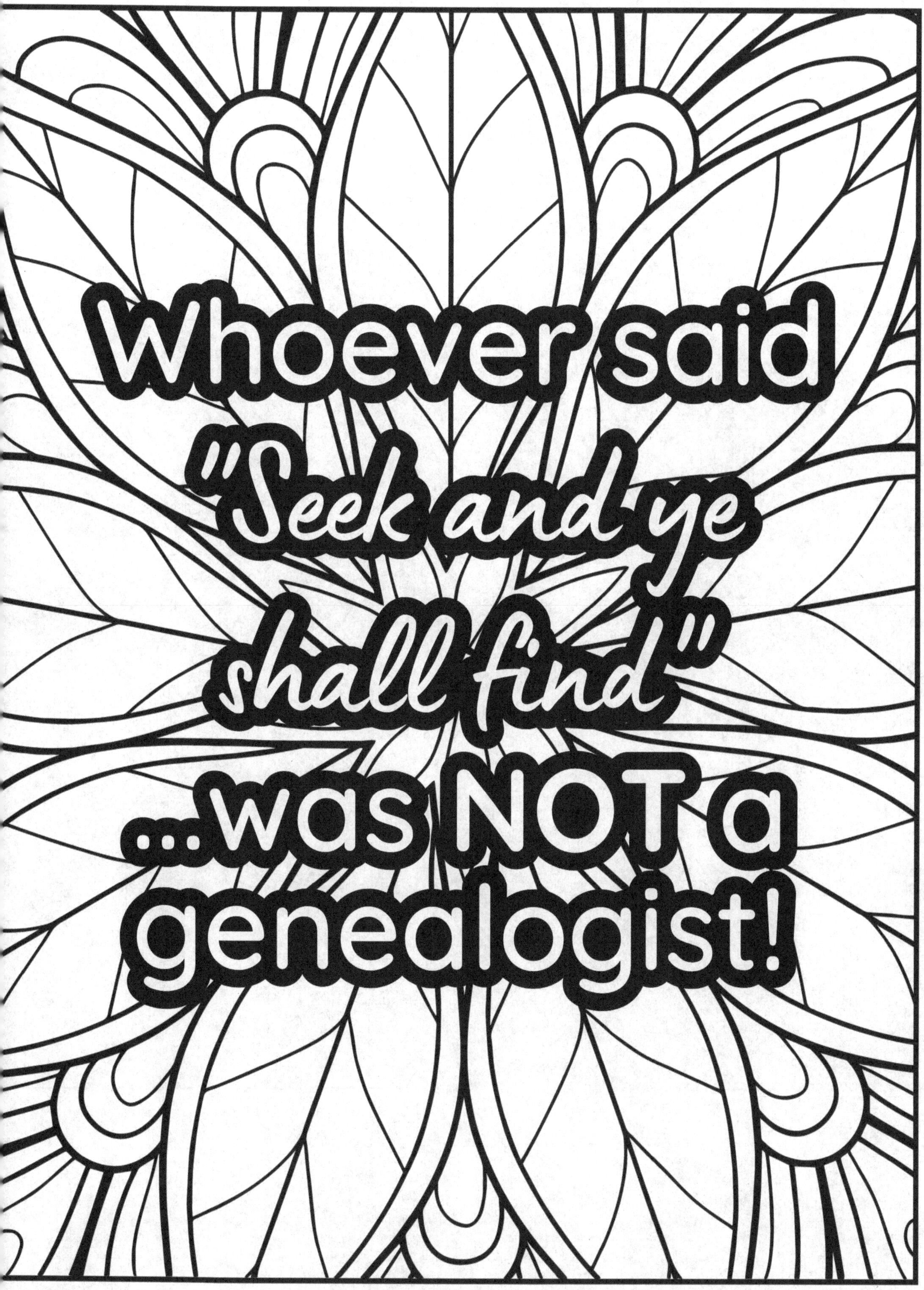
Whoever said
"Seek and ye
shall find"
...was NOT a
genealogist!

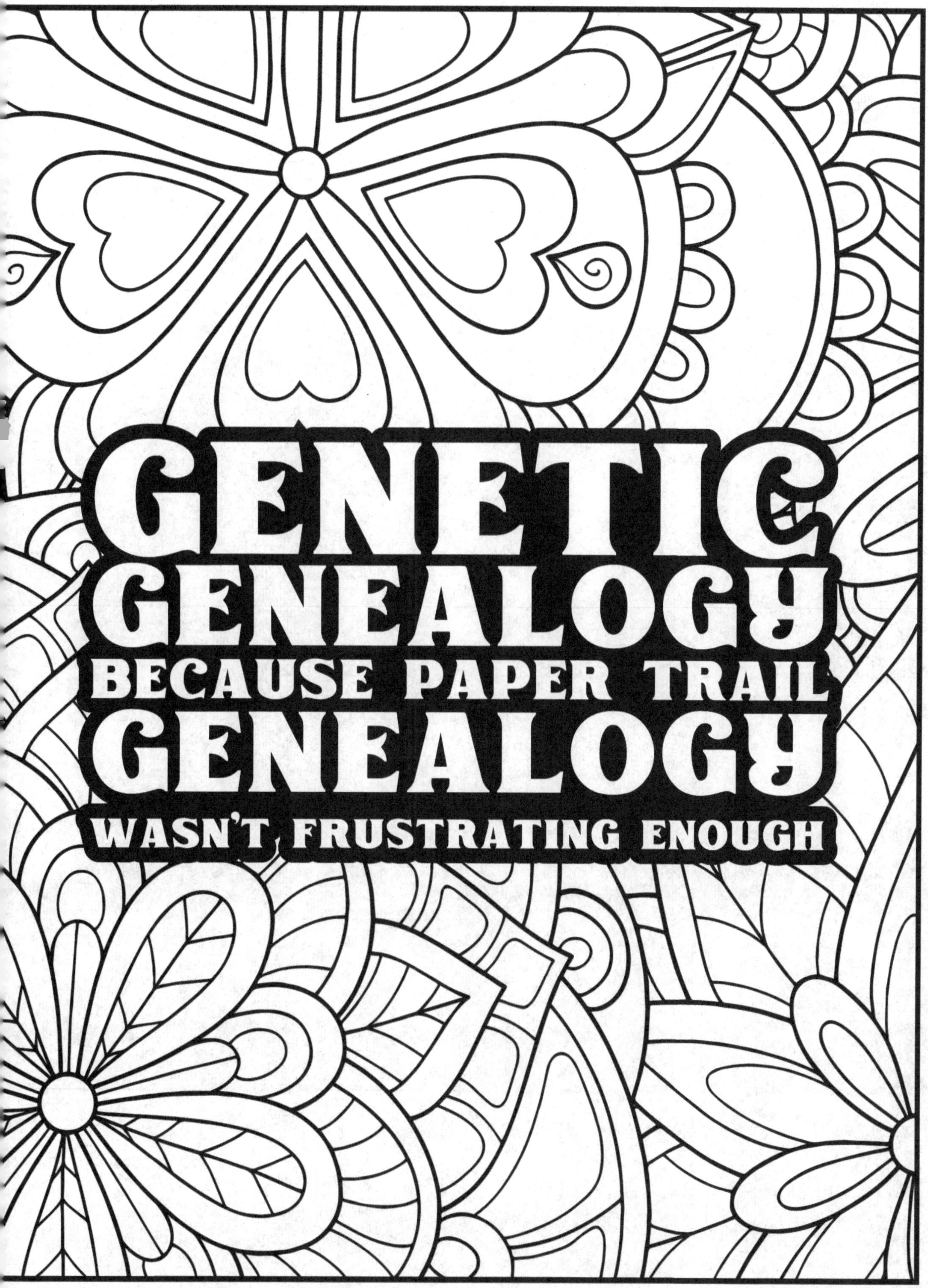
GENETIC
GENEALOGY
BECAUSE PAPER TRAIL
GENEALOGY
WASN'T FRUSTRATING ENOUGH

Made in United States
Troutdale, OR
12/14/2024

26466114R00038